Swedish Christmas Crafts

Helene S. Lundberg

Translated by Annika S. Hipple

Skyhorse Publishing

Skyhorse Publishing books may be purchased in bulk at special discounts for sales promotion, corporate gifts, fund raising, or educational purposes. Special editions can also be created to specifications. For details, contact the Special Sales Department, Skyhorse Publishing, 555 Eighth Avenue, Suite 903, New York, NY 10018 or info@skyhorsepublishing.com.

www.skyhorsepublishing.com

10 9 8 7 6 5 4 3 2 1

Library of Congress Cataloging-in-Publication Data
    Lundberg, Helene S.
    [Fint till jul. English]
    Swedish christmas crafts / Helene S. Lundberg.
        p.   cm.
    ISBN 978-1-60239-330-1 (alk. paper)
    1. Christmas decorations—Sweden.   I. Title.
TT900.C4L96   2008
745.594'1209485—dc22

2008020583

Printed in China

Contents

Preface

Swedish Christmas Crafts is intended to give you inspiration and ideas to make your home festive for Christmas. For me, the month before Christmas is especially nice with all the delicious food and fun things to do with family and friends. It's always exciting to dust off the Advent candleholder and set it out in its place of honor. So dig out the old reliable gingerbread and Lucia bun recipes, and let's get started on the Christmas preparations.

You shouldn't stress about Christmas. Think about what is important to you and your family, and put everything else aside for the time being.

The days leading up to Christmas are special, so relax and enjoy the season.

Christmasy jester's stocking

We all recognize the classic image of Christmas stockings hanging on the mantel, waiting for children to empty them on Christmas morning. These stockings will hold a few small packages, but most importantly, they are a lot of fun to make, not to mention how pretty they are.

This stocking is made with gorgeous purple felt and decorated with flowers. Who says you have to stick to traditional Christmas colors just because it's Christmas? It's always nice to have a splash of color that draws the eye. You can find felt and beads in a craft store or well-stocked fabric store. There are many colors to choose from, so don't be afraid to mix different colors and shades—there are no rules to follow. You will find the pattern for the stockings on the pattern pages.

Supplies needed:

Light purple felt, approximately 25.6 × 19.7 in (65 × 50 cm)
Dark purple felt for the flowers
Beads in different colors and sizes
Dark purple embroidery beads
Embroidery floss in two complementing shades
Embroidery needle
Scissors
Straight pins
Tracing paper and pen
Hand punch

What to do:

1 Trace the stocking (enlarge to 200%), the flower, and the felt button from pages 90–91 and 92 and cut them out of felt. You should cut out two stocking pieces, four flowers, and three buttons.

2 Pin the flowers to the front of the stocking and sew a big bead onto the middle of each flower.

3 Sew a ring of small beads around the big bead, but on the back side.

4 Sew chain stitches with the embroidery floss to make stems for the flowers.

5 Pin the sections of the stocking to one another and sew them together with simple stitches, starting approximately 4.7 in (12 cm) down on the forward part of the leg (the side with the toe).

6 Sew the beads onto the front of the stocking (see picture) at the same time as the simple stitches.

7 Sew the stocking pieces together until you have 9.4 in (24 cm) left on the rear part of the leg. Fold down the upper section and sew it down at the same time as you sew the stocking together.

8 Sew the buttons with two small beads on each.

9 Finish by sewing a row of beads along the edge of the fold, as shown in the picture.

Beige felt stocking

If you want a Christmas stocking that can hold a little more, perhaps this design will appeal to you. It's made out of beige felt and is decorated with beads, buttons, and embroidery. This is an easy one to personalize, so have fun!

This stocking looks great with all sorts of different decorations. Use buttons and beads in different sizes, and embroider with embroidery floss, pearl cotton, or thin crochet thread.

Sew the stocking together with simple whipstitches and embroider around the beads with stem stitching. Hang the stocking with a pretty matching velvet ribbon and decorate it with a complementing Christmas ornament. The pattern for the stocking is on page 91.

Supplies needed:

Beige felt, approximately 15.74 × 31.5 in
   (40 × 80 cm)
Small and large beads
Mother-of-pearl buttons
Embroidery floss in different colors
Velvet ribbon, approximately 39.4 in (1 m)
Sewing needle
Scissors
Tracing paper and pen
Hand punch

What to do:

1 Trace the stocking from the pattern page and cut out two stocking sections.

2 Draw on the decorations and sew on the beads.

3 Using embroidery floss or a similar thread, sew stem stitches around the beads.

4 Place the stocking sections with their back sides together and stitch them together. Attach the beads at the same time.

5 Make a hole in the upper part of the stocking with the hand punch and thread a velvet ribbon through the hole.

Little green stockings

Use green beads on this stocking to give it a little shimmer.

Attach the beads with double thread. The pattern for the stocking is on page 90, and should be enlarged to 200%.

Sew the sections of the stocking together with traditional buttonhole stitches; you can use either embroidery floss, pearl cotton, or cotton floss. On page 90, you can see how the buttonhole stitches should be sewn. Leave an opening at the upper front edge to sew on three buttons using the same thread. Make a hole in the stocking with a hand punch. Hang the stocking using a matching gros-grain ribbon.

Paper snowflakes

Remember those paper snowflakes from elementary school? Why not bring back old memories and use them for pretty window decorations? The impression of the snowflakes is enhanced if you also spray the edges of the window with artificial snow.

You can use just about any type of paper. The larger snowflake is made from slightly heavier paper and the smaller ones with a fine, patterned paper. Any craft or specialty paper store will have an abundance of attractive and unusual paper. Experiment with different shapes and patterns—a heart looks nice in the snowy window. Working with a craft knife is also effective.

Supplies needed:
Paper
Small scissors or craft knife, a cutting mat, and a steel ruler

What to do:
1 Decide which shape you want for your snowflake. If you're making a heart, start by folding the paper in the middle, and then cut out half a heart.

2 Fold a few more times.

3 Cut small slits, circles, half-moons, etc.

Felt hearts

This is a good way to make gingerbread hearts that stay fresh year after year. These cute hearts are made from a lovely thick felt, in true gingerbread color. These are perfect for hanging on a door or in a window, and if you make them smaller, they're just the right size for hanging on the Christmas tree.

You can find this thick type of felt in most major craft stores. Buttons are one of my big passions, so I always decorate the heart with a pretty button. Gluing it on instead of sewing it keeps the back side clean. If you want a heart that's decorated on both sides, sew buttons back to back, one on either side of the felt. I always buy buttons when I'm traveling—I found these in a supermarket in Prague!

Supplies needed:
Thick brown felt
Red-and-white striped ribbon
Decorative buttons
Hand punch
Craft glue
Tracing paper and pen
Pins
Scissors

What to do:

1 Trace the heart from page 93 onto a piece of paper and cut it out.

2 Pin the paper heart to the felt and cut around the pattern.

3 Make a hole in the felt heart with the hand punch.

4 Attach the button with craft glue; allow the glue to dry thoroughly before continuing.

5 Thread the ribbon through the hole and hang.

Stars . . .

A simple and classic decoration that's suitable both in windows and on mirrors. Stick with traditional Christmas colors, or get wild, it's all up to you.

Choose a sturdy paper so that the stars will hang neatly on the ribbon. Copy the star from page 92 onto a heavy piece of paper to use as a pattern. Draw the stars according to your pattern and cut them out.

Make a small hole with a hand punch in the middle of each star. Thread the ribbon on a darning needle and pull the needle and ribbon through the stars. Pull the stars into place and hang the garland using tape.

. . . and dots

Using round self-adhesive labels (easily available at any craft or office supply store) and some thread, you can easily make a pretty snowfall for any window in the house.

Use either fishing line or regular white sewing thread to attach the labels. Stick the labels to each other with the thread in between. This is a great activity for younger kids who want to help you decorate. Place the snowflakes as close together or as far apart as you wish.

When you are finished, attach the strings of snowflakes to the window frame. They are so light that a piece of tape is sufficient to hang them with.

Christmas greetings

It's always fun to get a beautifully wrapped present. Sometimes it's so nicely done that you almost don't want to open it, but curiosity always wins out. I think it's just as fun, if not more so, to give a beautiful package. It's worth a lot to see how happy it makes the recipient. It's always nice to match packages with cards in the same style. Make the package and the card as personalized as possible—everyone likes to get something homemade.

Pretty stamp prints

Have you tried this new embossing technique? If not, it's time to do so. The prints will have an attractive raised surface that looks professionally done. Stamp directly on the cards and packages or cut around the prints to use them as labels or decorations.

During the holiday season, most craft stores carry a large selection of stamps. You'll also find embossing powder, which gives the print a raised, shiny surface after heating. Use a slightly heavier, high-quality paper for a nice, profes-sional appearance. Remember, don't use a regu-lar hair dryer for your embossing project; the air will blow the powder away. Use a special heat tool instead.

You'll find the heat tool in the craft store, where you'll also find all the supplies you need. One alternative to the heat tool is to use an ordinary stove. Hold the paper over a warm burner until the powder has melted—but watch your fingers!

There's even a special embossing pen that you can use to write personalized greetings on your Christmas cards, which works the same way as the stamps.

Supplies needed:
Stamp or embossing pen
Stamp pad
Embossing powder
Paper
Heat tool

What to do:
1 Press the stamp carefully to the stamp pad, making sure the whole stamp absorbs the ink.

2 Stamp the paper, pressing evenly so that the whole stamp print comes out.

3 Pour on plenty of embossing powder—do this quickly before the stamp print has time to dry.

4 Shake the paper with the powder so that the powder is distributed over the entire stamp. Pour the extra powder back into the jar.

5 Carefully heat the stamp print with the heat tool or over the stove burner until the powder melts. Allow it to cool before continuing.

3-D tree cards

This card isn't difficult, and you can make your own creations by swapping the designs and colors.

Start with 8½ × 11 in card stock, and then fold it in half, as shown in the picture. The gold paper is 3.9 × 3.9 in (10 × 10 cm). For the tree, use small glass decorating balls or beads, but if you can't find them small enough, glitter will work. Both stick easily to the adhesive sheets, and remember to hold the paper over a bowl to catch anything that doesn't stick, so you can use it later.

The mounting tape is also double-sided and adds an attractive and professional touch to your cards.

Supplies needed:
Red and gold card stock
Double-sided adhesive sheets
Small decorating balls or glitter
White rhinestones
Double-sided mounting tape
Scissors or craft knife
Pen and ruler
Craft glue

What to do:
1 Cut the red and gold card stock according to the dimensions described above.

2 Transfer the tree pattern from page 92 to a double-sided adhesive sheet and cut it out.

3 Peel off the protective paper on one side of the adhesive sheet and place the tree in the middle of the gold-colored card stock.

4 Peel off the protective paper from the other side and sprinkle the small decorating balls or glitter on the surface. Press lightly with your hand so that they stick.

5 Glue the white rhinestones to the ends of the tree branches and allow the card to dry.

6 Tape the piece of gold-colored card stock on a half-folded red card, using the mounting tape to obtain an attractive 3-D effect.

7 Do the same thing for the package, but place the double-sided adhesive sheet directly on the package.

Hearty greetings

Decorating cards and packages with hearts is always appreciated. For these cards, I've used small decorating balls in two different colors. The red balls have the same color as the card itself, creating a pure and striking impression.

For these cards, I've chosen an attractive and elegant paper with stripes, but you should choose whatever you think looks best. Be sure to use a paper that is sturdy and substantial, because it will be easier to work with. I've also added a heart-shaped window to one card, and included the pattern for it on page 92.

Supplies needed:

Red card stock
Double-sided adhesive sheets
Scissors
Craft knife
Small decorating balls or glitter
Ruler
Pen

What to do:

1 Transfer the heart from the pattern pages to a double-sided adhesive sheet and cut it out.

2 Fold the red card stock, remove the protective paper from one side of the adhesive sheet, and attach the hearts in a row.

3 Pull off the protective paper from the other side of one heart at a time and sprinkle on the small decorating balls or glitter.

4 Press lightly with your hand so that they stick to the adhesive sheet.

5 On the left side of the card, draw the outline of a heart and cut it out with the craft knife.

6 Attach a self-adhesive heart at the same height as the heart-shaped window and pour on the small decorating balls.

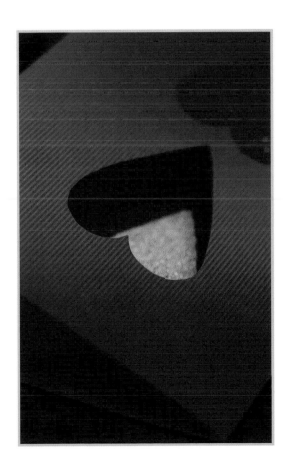

Stars in relief

I find that people are drawn to this naturally colored package with matching cards and address labels. They are just as fun to make as to receive, and it's hard to throw away the paper after the package has been opened; if you're careful you might be able to reuse it.

The stars have been decorated with a glaze pen. Here I've used a white one, but if you prefer a more glamorous style, most craft stores have glaze pens in colors like metallic gold. Be sure to let the glaze dry thoroughly before you put the card in the envelope or attach the label to the package.

Supplies needed:

Brown packaging paper
Handmade watercolor paper
Glue stick
Glaze pen
Scissors
Pen
Hand punch
Natural-colored cord

What to do:
Cards and address labels

1 Fold a piece of handmade watercolor paper down the middle.

2 Transfer stars in different sizes onto the brown packaging paper and cut them out.

3 Using a glue stick, glue the stars to the watercolor paper. For best results, place it in a press for a while so that the glue has time to dry.

4 Apply the glaze pen to the stars to make dots, lines, or other patterns. Allow them to dry.

5 Make a hole with the hand punch on the length side of the card. Thread a cord through the hole and tie it together.

6 To cut out the labels, use the pattern on page 92.

The package

1 Wrap the present in brown packaging paper.

2 Draw stars directly on the paper and fill in the outlines with the glaze pen.

"Angels—do they exist?"

Use angels as a theme when you make your own Christmas cards for relatives, friends, and acquaintances. Aren't they charming? I think they give a special feeling to all gatherings around Christmas. These cards also make pretty wall hangings, so make a couple extra for yourself.

Here you can use just about any materials you like; it's fun to experiment. I have made the cards using various techniques and different materials. Angels are found in so many different places: napkins, wrapping and tissue paper, decorative ribbons, and wallpaper. Collect them throughout the year so that you have some things to choose from when the Christmas card making gets going. Complement the angels with matching ribbons and other pretty decorations.

Supplies needed:

White card stock
Angel-themed material (napkin, wrapping paper, wallpaper, etc.)
Gold matte paper
Rice paper in various brown shades
Gold heart gems
Scissors or craft knife
Glue stick or double-sided tape
Craft glue
Ruler

What to do:

1 Divide a sheet of white 8½ x 11 in card stock in such a way that you get a card of the size you want.

2 Spread a thin layer of glue on the card stock and press on the rice paper. Smooth it with your hand and, for best results, place the paper in a press so that it dries. Fold it down the middle.

3 Cut a piece of gold-colored matte paper and glue it onto the middle of the card.

4 Tear out an angel motif from, for example, a napkin. Use only the top layer.

5 Glue the image to the card; place it in a press.

6 Finish by attaching some hearts using the craft glue.

Supplies needed:

White card stock
Wide angel ribbon
Bookmark
Gold cording
Glue stick
Scissors and craft knife
Pen and ruler
Double-sided mounting tape

What to do:

Window card

1 Fold a white piece of card stock down the middle. Cut a square somewhat smaller than the size of the card when half-folded. (This piece will be placed inside the window.)

2 Draw and cut a square on the left side of the card. (Draw on the inside of the card, so you don't have to worry about the lines being visible when the card is done.)

3 Place the square piece of card stock in the half-folded card, position the bookmark, and glue the bookmark to the square.

4 Glue a piece of gold cording onto the square on either side of the bookmark.

5 Pull off the protective paper on the double-sided mounting tape, and attach the square with the bookmark to the left side of the card inside the window.

Ribbon card

1 This card is quick and easy to put together. Follow step 1 as for the card above.

2 Cut the wide angel ribbon approximately 3 cm (1.2 in) longer than the height of the card.

3 Holding the glue stick directly over the card, glue the ribbon onto the card, continuing on the back side of the card.

4 To hide the ends of the ribbon, glue a piece of card stock to the inside of the card.

Supplies needed:

Beige paper with gold flecks
Finished envelope
Heavy card stock, .4–.6 in (1–1.5 cm) thick
Tissue paper printed with angels
Glue stick
Double-sided tape
Scissors and craft knife
Pen and ruler

What to do:

1 Fold the beige paper to the desired size of your card. For example, you can fold an 8½ × 11 in sheet of paper directly down the middle or divide it before folding it.

2 Cut the heavy card stock to a size proportionate to that of the card.

3 Cut a square of the angel-patterned tissue paper.

4 Spread glue onto the card stock and press the tissue paper onto it. Place some glue on the back of the card stock and smooth down the paper. Allow it to dry before continuing.

5 Attach the decoration with the double-sided tape directly to the half-folded card.

Children's Christmas cards

It's fun when a homemade Christmas card arrives in the mailbox, especially when the greeting comes from the younger members of the family. A pleasant way to spend time with your children is to gather around the dining table to make the year's Christmas cards. It's a joy to see how they cut, glue, and paint their little masterpieces without inhibitions.

To keep the kids interested, set out a variety of supplies, which can include everything from ordinary white paper to glitter and paint pens. Then it's just a matter of getting the creative process started. Make sure the kids are interested in project, and keep it fun!

Supplies needed:

Paper of different qualities and colors
Double-sided adhesive sheets
Glitter
Ribbon
Stickers
Gold and silver pens
Pens in different colors

What to do:

White card with line drawing

1 Fold a sturdy piece of paper down the middle to create a half-fold card.

2 Cut a piece of gold-colored paper so that it is a few millimeters smaller than the card.

3 Divide another piece of white paper in such a way that it fits the card.

4 Let the children draw line drawings however they want on the white paper.

5 Attach the drawing to gold paper and then tape the gold paper directly to the card. For best results, use double-sided tape.

6 Feel free to make a nice address label in the same style.

Glitter cards

1 Cut out hearts from the double-sided adhesive sheets and attach them directly to single or folded cards.

2 Sprinkle plenty of glitter and press it down with your fingers so that it sticks.

3 Shake off the excess glitter and pour it back into the jar so that it lasts longer.

Eye candy

Creating appealing and eye-catching decorations for Christmas is always popular and fun. For most people, Christmas is a time for community and relaxation, so it's extra important to make one's surroundings cozy and comfortable, and it doesn't have to be difficult to create the right atmosphere.

Eye-catching decorations

Buy some extra-large mistletoe, so there's enough to make a decorative wreath to brighten up the wall. Did you know that mistletoe is actually a weed that can sometimes grow so large on other trees that the trees don't survive? Mistletoe has a wonderful green color and stays pretty for a long time, even if it dries out.

You can create another pretty and eye-catching decoration by placing some pillar candles in a row on a platter. Cut spruce twigs and arrange them around the candles. Feel free to decorate the twigs with something Christmasy—here I've placed two red ceramic hearts loosely on top. You can make the wreath easily by following the steps on pages 46–47.

Christmas smells

For me, one of the most delicious smells of Christmas is the mix of orange, cloves, and cinnamon. Make little colorful and aromatic groups and place them on a suitable platter. They are as nice to look at as they are to smell. This is a good craft that is appreciated by all ages, so why not gather the whole family around the kitchen table?

You can use oranges, mandarins, or clementines for this project. Personally I think the oranges smell the best, but the smaller fruits can be more attractive on a table. If it's hard to get the cloves into the fruit you can use an awl or a darning needle to make little holes. Just don't make the holes too big, or the cloves might fall out.

Supplies needed:
Oranges, mandarins, or clementines
Whole cloves
Cinnamon sticks
Matching ribbon

What to do:
1 Press the cloves into the oranges, mandarins, or clementines, making a simple pattern.

2 Gather together some nice-looking cinnamon sticks and tie them together with a pretty ribbon.

3 Place the fruit and the cinnamon bunches on a glass dish or other suitable surface.

Colorful Christmas crackers

Christmas crackers might sound a bit silly, but they most definitely are not. Gather them together on a pretty dish, or use them as a decoration or place card on the Christmas table. Delight in glorious colors; there are so many fun materials you can use. Decorate them with colorful glass rhinestones, for example.

As the foundation for Christmas crackers, I use ordinary empty toilet paper rolls. If you want really long crackers, you can use empty paper towel rolls. For best results, use colored tissue paper for the cracker itself and heavier paper for the decoration. Tie the tissue paper with a matching ribbon. As an extra decoration you can glue on colored glass rhinestones with flat backs.

Supplies needed:

Empty paper rolls
Tissue paper
Decorative paper
Colored glass rhinestones with flat backs
Satin ribbon
Double-sided tape
Small scissors
Craft glue
Pen and ruler

What to do:

1 Place the paper roll 4.7 in (12 cm) from the edge of the tissue paper and mark the ends of the roll.

2 Cut the tissue paper so that it is 4.7 in (12 cm) wider on either side of the roll and long enough that you can wrap it around the roll 3–5 times.

3 Slowly fold the paper lengthwise like an accordion, approximately 3.9 in (10 cm) in from each side, and cut approximately .4 in (1 cm) wide slits in the accordion.

4 Roll the paper roll in the tissue paper and fasten the ends with double-sided tape.

5 Cut a piece of the decorative paper, slightly smaller than the roll itself and long enough that

there is some overlap on the roll. Fold the paper and cut out a simple pattern with the small scissors.

6 Attach the paper cutout with the double-sided tape.

7 Tie the ends together with matching satin ribbon.

8 Finish by gluing a rhinestone or similar decoration on the cracker.

Soft hearts

Hearts in all shapes and materials are an integral part of Christmas. Here are two varieties of soft hearts that look great on a door or cabinet. While you're at it, take the opportunity to make a few extra; they're perfect as gifts!

The hearts are made of felt, which is a fun material to work with. Decorate them with simple stitches, buttons, and gems. You can embroider them with either thin woolen or cotton thread. Sew them together with decorative buttonhole stitches and fill them with stuffing. The pattern for the heart can be found on page 93.

Supplies needed:

Felt
Woolen thread
Embroidery needle
Gem or button
Stuffing
Pins
Scissors
French chalk
Tracing paper

What to do:

1 Transfer the heart from the pattern page and cut out two hearts from the felt.

2 Draw patterns on the heart with the colored French chalk and sew simple stitches in the outlines. If desired, sew on a gem or button.

3 Pin the two parts together with the back sides together.

4 Sew them together with buttonhole stitches. When 2 in remain, fill the heart with the stuffing and then sew the opening shut.

5 Thread a bit of woolen thread through the upper side of the heart and hang the heart in a suitable place.

Elegant wreaths

It has become an annual tradition for me to make small wreaths that I hang on all the kitchen cabinets for Advent. Everyone who sees them says they are so sweet and Christmasy. Hang them with a classic red-and-white striped ribbon. With matching candle rings the kitchen is just about ready for Christmas—now it's just the snow we're waiting for.

You can use different kinds of greens to decorate the wreaths. For best results, choose something with robust leaves, which will stay fresh longer. It's best to make the framework for the wreath yourself so that you can get the right size for the spot where you're going to hang it. Make the framework out of elephant wire, a soft annealed steel wire that's

easy to shape and work with. Iron wire is also annealed; use it to fasten the elephant wire. Florist wire, also known as "myrtle wire," is a very thin wire that's available in different colors, so it won't be visible on the wreath. On the next page you'll see just how to go about making your own wreaths.

Make your own Christmas wreath

It's not at all difficult to make your own Christmas wreath, and by doing it yourself, you can decide the shape and size of your wreath. You can even make a heart-shaped or elliptical wreath. It's just a matter of shaping the wire the way you want it. The supplies are sufficient for several wreaths, so why not get your friends together for a cozy evening of crafts?

Supplies needed:

Elephant wire
Iron wire
Florist tape
Wire cutters
Florist wire
Pruning shears
Ribbon
Real or artificial greenery

What to do:

1 Fasten two elephant wires together by wrapping their overlapping ends tightly with the iron wire (see picture).

2 Shape the elephant wire either freely or around something that is the same size as the wreath you want to make (see picture).

3 Attach the other ends with the iron wire and make sure they are securely fastened.

4 Wrap the wreath framework with florist tape. Pull on the tape as you dress the wreath (see picture).

5 Cut the greens into smaller pieces. Approximately 5 cm (2 in) is usually suitable (see picture).

6 Wrap the florist wire a few times around the wreath frame so that it is properly attached.

7 Hold 2–3 small sprigs of greens around the wreath frame and wrap them with the florist wire to fasten. About 3 times around is usually sufficient (see picture).

8 Continue around the whole wreath and finish by wrapping the florist wire around the wreath frame a few extra times.

On the Christmas tree

Every year our tree at home changes its appearance, and it's not about trends but simply about feelings. Sometimes you might feel like having a traditionally decorated tree with lots of red, green, and gold. Other years you might want to use a single color on the tree, to give it a simple and modern style. The important thing is to create a personalized tree that everyone in the family likes.

White on the tree

Artificial trees have found their way into many homes, and they're certainly great if you can't have a real tree due to allergies or other reasons. But nothing compares to the real kind, with the delicious smell of newly cut spruce spreading through the room.

It's a fun tradition to go as a family to cut your own tree. Bring a thermos of hot chocolate—it can be a great day in the woods. Check your local newspaper for ads about where you can cut your own tree. We decorated our tree in white this year, but the following decorations can be done in any color to suit your tree. There are many fun Christmas decorations that you can

easily make yourself. Feel free to get some help from the family—it can be a nice time around the kitchen table. Here you can see some examples of Christmas decorations that you can make yourself. If you're making several of each, it's easiest to make a pattern of sturdy paper that you can use several times.

Fabric tree
Supplies needed:

White fabric
Stuffing
Thin satin ribbon
White beads
Sewing needle and thread
Pins
Paper for the pattern
Pen

What to do:

1 Transfer the tree from page 92 to the pattern paper. Fold the material in half, pin the pattern to the fabric, and cut it out.

2 Cut the satin ribbon; you'll need approximately 5.1 in (13 cm) for one tree.

3 Place the trees face-to-face with the satin ribbon between them at the top of the tree.

4 Sew the trees together by machine but leave an opening on one side.

5 Fill the tree with stuffing and sew the opening shut by hand with small stitches.

6 Sew on the beads on both sides and fasten the thread on the side.

Paper heart
Supplies needed:

White card stock
Scissors or craft knife
Sewing thread
Sewing needle
Paper for the pattern
Pencil
Hand punch (optional)

What to do:

1 Make a pattern from the heart on page 94.

2 Trace the heart lightly on the white card stock, as many times as you want.

3 Cut out the hearts with a small pair of scissors or a craft knife.

4 Thread the sewing needle with approximately 5 in of thread and poke it through the top side of the heart, or use a hand punch to make a small hole for the thread. Tie the ends together and hang the heart.

Beaded heart
Supplies needed:

Thin steel wire
Beads
Side cutter pliers
Round nose pliers
Sewing thread

What to do:

1 Using the side cutters, cut a piece of wire approximately 11 in long.

2 Fold the wire down the middle to make the pointy end of the heart.

3 Shape the rounded arches of the heart.

4 Thread beads over one of the arches and make sure to push them all the way to the point.

5 Using the round nose pliers, shape a loop when one side is finished.

6 Thread beads on the other side and finish by threading the end through the loop and fastening it.

7 Hang the heart by threading the thread through the loop.

Star
Supplies needed:

White card stock
Metallic silver glaze pen
Scissors or craft knife
Sewing thread
Sewing needle
Paper for pattern
Pencil
Hand punch (optional)

What to do:

1 Make a pattern using the star on page 92.

2 Using the pencil, trace the star lightly onto the card stock, as many times as you want.

3 Cut out the shapes using a small pair of scissors or a craft knife.

4 Write text using a metallic silver glaze pen (optional). Allow it to dry completely before continuing.

5 Thread the sewing needle with approximately 5 in of thread and poke it through the upper point of the star, or use a hand punch to make a small hole for the thread. If you like, thread a bead on the double thread. Tie the ends together and hang the star.

Renew the red ornaments

Are you tired of your old Christmas tree ornaments? No problem—it's a piece of cake to freshen them up. With decorations and ribbons, they'll be as good as new. Here you'll find some examples of things you can do with them. Look in your drawers at home or check the craft store—there's a wealth of materials that you can use to work wonders.

To make things easier while you're decorating Christmas tree ornaments, you should hold onto the shaft of the ball if it's well attached. If this part is removable, it's best to take it off, place the ball on a pen, and hold onto the pen while you decorate the ball. Allow the decorations to dry completely before attaching the satin ribbon and hanging the ornament on the tree.

Supplies needed:

Christmas tree ornaments
Sequins
Craft glue
Purple glaze pen
Purple glitter
Paintbrush
Satin ribbon

What to do:

1 Sequined ornament. Apply dots of craft glue to the ornament and press on the sequins. If you have a hard time handling the small sequins, you can pick them up with the help of a pencil.

2 Relief ornament. Make dots all over the ornament using a glaze pen and allow them to dry completely.

3 Glitter ornament. Brush a thin layer of craft glue over a small area of the ornament. Spread on plenty of glitter; be sure to place a sheet of paper underneath so that you can easily collect all the excess glitter.

Colorful Christmas tree decorations

Making Christmas tree decorations out of paper is simple and fun. Use some unusual colors that aren't so common in a traditional tree—why not decorate your tree in orange this year?

These two orange decorations are sewn together by machine. If you don't have a sewing machine, you can sew them together by hand; it takes a bit longer, but the end result is just as good. Decorate the paper figures with whatever you have at home. For these, I've used a metallic gold glaze pen and beads, together with a thin gold-colored metal wire. Search in your drawers; you've probably got lots of small things you can use. The patterns for the figures can be found on pages 94–95.

Supplies needed:

Paper
Needle and thread
Beads
Metal wire
Glaze pen
Scissors or craft knife
Hand punch for the Christmas tree

What to do:

Orange prism

1 Transfer the prism from page 95 to a paper pattern and cut out five identical parts.
2 Place the parts on top of each other. Pull out a bit of thread from the sewing machine before you sew them together down the middle with a straight machine stitch. Pull out some extra thread at the end before you cut it.
3 Thread a bead at the point of the prism and anchor it with some knots. Also tie up the upper thread.
4 Fold out the parts and press lightly with your hand.

Orange cone with gold decoration

1 Cut out two cones of paper. Sew them together in the same way as the prism.
2 Fold and press out the parts and decorate them with a metallic gold glaze pen.

Red Christmas tree with beads

1 Cut a tree out of sturdy paper, using the pattern on page 95.
2 Make small holes with the hand punch: one at the top, one at the bottom, and one on each branch.
3 Anchor the metal wire in the lower part of the tree, thread on the beads, and fasten them by entwining them in the metal wire.
4 Thread the metal wire through the holes, and along the back of the tree. Anchor it at the top.

Romantic baskets

You probably recognize the shape of the classic baskets, but here is one with a more modern design. You can shape and decorate them any way you like so that they fit your own tree. Hang them on the tree with or without goodies inside.

Here you can use just about any type of paper, and there certainly are a lot of attractive kinds to choose from. It's perfectly fine to mix different weights and colors; the final result can vary greatly.

Supplies needed:

Paper in different colors
Decorations (such as wrapping paper,
    cutouts from magazines, etc.)
Glaze pen
Hand punch
Plate or similar item for pattern
Pen
Scissors
Glue stick or double-sided tape

What to do:

1 Use a plate as a pattern and draw two circles. Cut them out.

2 Fold the circles down the middle and attach them to one another (see picture).

3 Decorate the basket.

4 Cut a strip of paper in proportion to the basket and glue it to the inside of the basket as a handle.

5 Make holes with the hand punch along the edge or make small dots with a glaze pen.

Cones and crackers

Why not add some music to your Christmas tree this year? After all, music is an important part of Christmas. Fill the cone with nuts or candy and the crackers with goodies. Music paper adds a homey, festive atmosphere to your tree.

If you don't have a book of music that you're willing to sacrifice, you can buy loose sheet music at the craft or paper store. Use either tissue paper or, as I've done here, parchment paper for the stuffing. Hang the cone and the Christmas cracker with a matching ribbon of satin, velvet, or silk. Feel free to use double-sided tape to close the cone or cracker. Make the Christmas cracker as described on page 41.

Supplies needed:

Music paper
Tissue or parchment paper
Double-sided tape
Scissors
Stapler
Pen
Ribbon

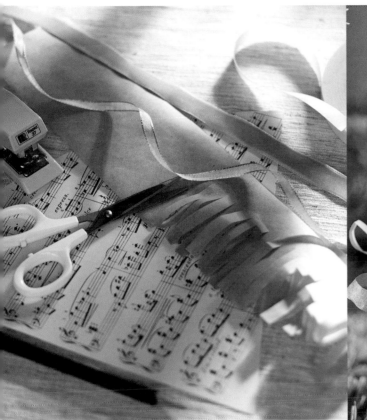

What to do:

1 Transfer the cone from page 96 to the music paper and cut it out.

2 Attach a strip of double-sided tape along one side, remove the protective plastic, and roll the paper into a cone.

3 Fold half of the parchment paper lengthwise and cut several slits.

4 Attach it to the inside of the cone using the stapler.

5 Cut a piece of ribbon approximately 40 in long to hang the cone. Fasten it to the front side of the cone and allow it to hang loose along the sides of the cone.

6 Place a piece of double-sided tape along the sides and fasten the ribbon in it to hide the staples.

Pastels on the tree

Personally I think these decorations came out the prettiest; they feel new and trendy. Not to mention how fun and simple they were to throw together. Match paper and sequins or mix things up a bit. The final result can be very striking, and it's always fun to try some new methods.

I found this paper in the craft store; it's an iridescent mother-of-pearl paper that is sturdy and easy to work with. Even the sequins are iridescent and come in many different colors. You can find them at your craft or sewing store. The decorations are hung using embroidery floss. It's easiest either to use a small pair of scissors or a craft knife and cutting mat. You can find the patterns on pages 92 and 94–95.

Supplies needed:

Iridescent mother-of-pearl paper
Iridescent sequins
Glue stick
Embroidery floss
Craft glue
Scissors
Craft knife (optional)
Pen
Card stock for pattern

What to do:

1 Transfer the star, heart, and crown shapes to a heavyweight paper that you can use as a pattern. Cut them out.

2 Trace the shapes onto the mother-of-pearl paper. You will need two of each. Cut them out.

3 Cut the embroidery floss, approximately 5 in for each shape.

4 Fold the floss down the middle. Glue the shapes together back to back, with the floss in between them.

5 For best results, place the paper in a press for a few minutes until the glue has dried and the shape is nice and smooth.

6 Glue sequins to both sides of the figure using the craft glue. Use only a minimal amount for each sequin to avoid excess stickiness. Pick up the sequins using a pen if it's difficult to manage by hand.

The candles of Christmas

Christmas is the time for candles. There's something special about lighting a candle; the atmosphere immediately becomes cozy and homey. Personally I always have a candle lit during the darker time of year while I'm cooking. It makes things more festive at home and gives me inspiration in the kitchen. There are many different styles of candleholder, but I think the best and most attractive ones are those you make yourself. Take a look at the next chapter and get inspired.

Lucia wreath and apples

Both the Lucia wreath and beautiful red apples make ideal candleholders. They are perfect to have on a rustic and traditionally set Christmas table. Thanks to their low height, they don't block the line of sight for the guests. Make some extras and place them on your Christmas buffet; it's always nice to keep the same style through the whole dinner.

Use small taper candles for both the Lucia wreath and the apples. Otherwise, there's a risk that the candles will become loose. The apples may not be very long-lived, but they will stay fresh for at least one of the days of Christmas. The Lucia wreath, on the other hand, can last for ages, as long as it isn't placed in a plastic bag. I still have mine, which has dried and is just as attractive as in the picture.

Advent candleholder

Have you also tired of your old traditional Advent candleholder? Do what I do and look in your drawers. You'll probably find something that you can use as an Advent candleholder. It can be just as personalized as you like. These little zinc flowerpots and the saucer lay discarded in the greenhouse, and they weren't doing much good there at this time of year.

It's nice to use pillar candles for the Advent candleholder. At our house, the candles burn down too quickly, so we always have to switch and move the candles all the time. With the bigger pillar candles, we can let them burn in peace and quiet without worrying that they'll burn out before Christmas Eve. The pots are filled with sand and gravel to hold the candles in place.

Supplies needed:
Zinc saucer with pots
Sand and gravel
Red wax sheet
Craft knife
Pen

What to do:

1 Draw numbers directly onto the wax sheet. You can print numbers off the computer to help you, but remember that you may need to make them mirror images.

2 Cut out the numbers with a craft knife.

3 Remove the protective paper from the wax sheet and attach the numbers directly to the candles. Hold your hand over them and press lightly so that they stick.

4 Pour a little sand in the bottom of the pots. Hold the candles in the middle of the pots and fill them with sand and gravel. Now the Advent celebrations can begin.

Snow candles

Enjoy the feeling of snow even inside in the warm comfort of the house. Snow and Christmas go together, in my opinion—there's no real Christmas without snow. Coarse salt is the perfect indoor substitution for snow. It's great for holding small candles in place, and it certainly creates a striking and Christmasy impression.

You've most likely got a lot of stuff at home in your kitchen cabinets that would work well as candle molds. A recycled glass jam jar can be very pretty with just a little imagination. In this way you can change your home as often as you like without spending a fortune. The little zinc molds are actually old baking tins. Open your cabinets at home, and you'll probably find lots of things that will work. Fill the molds or jars with coarse salt and then press in either tea lights or short pillar candles. Feel free to decorate with a pretty ribbon, but don't forget to think about fireproofing.

Simple lanterns

Use ordinary drinking glasses or glass jars and turn them into pretty lanterns. While you're at it, why not make a few extras? It's very practical to have a few presents handy for when you're invited to someone's home.

Is there anything nicer than receiving something homemade as a gift? Wash and clean the glasses thoroughly before decorating them. These lanterns are decorated in three different ways; decide which degree of difficulty and style suits you best. You'll find all the supplies in your craft store.

Angel lantern
Supplies needed:

Glass jar
Napkin with angel motif
Scissors
Decoupage varnish for glass
Glaze pen for writing on glass
Paintbrush

What to do:

1 From a napkin, cut out a design of a suitable shape and size for your jar. Use only the top layer of the napkin.
2 Spread some decoupage varnish on the glass jar, place the napkin design on the varnish, and gently smooth it with a paintbrush. Be careful so that the napkin doesn't tear.
3 Allow the napkin and jar to dry slightly before brushing them with another layer of decoupage varnish.
4 When the jar and design have dried, paint the outline with a gold glaze pen made for writing on glass.
5 Dab dots all over the jar. Allow to dry before using.

Transparent lantern
Supplies needed:

Glass
Decorative vellum or rice paper
Scissors
Double-sided tape

What to do:

1 Cut the vellum or rice paper to the same height as the glass and approximately .5 in longer than the circumference of the glass.

2 Fasten the double-sided tape at the short end, shape the paper around the glass, and attach the ends.

Star lantern
Supplies needed:

Glass jar
Handmade watercolor paper
Darning needle or similar tool
Double-sided tape
Styrofoam or similar material
Scissors

What to do:

1 Cut a piece of watercolor paper slightly higher than the glass jar and approximately 0.8 in (2 cm) longer than the circumference of the jar.

2 Draw a pattern on the reverse side. You may be able to use something from the pattern pages.

3 Poke holes along the lines with a darning needle or other sharp object. Use a Styrofoam board or similar surface underneath, so that you can press the needle through. Feel free to make holes of various sizes.

4 Place double-sided tape along the short edge of the watercolor paper, shape the paper around the glass jar, and attach the overlapping ends with the double-sided tape.

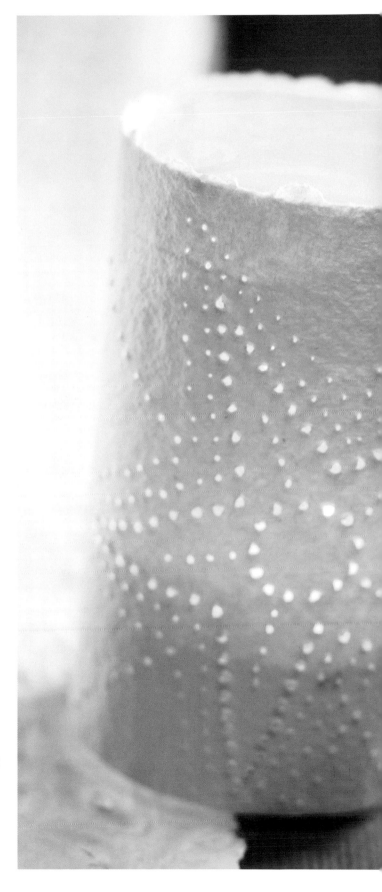

Candleholder with beads

Is there anything more festive than live candles in the tree, especially in such a pretty candle-holder? Make one or more and hang them in your tree. The beaded candleholder takes some time to make, but you will be able to enjoy it for many years to come. No doubt it will be admired and appreciated by all your Christmas guests.

The most important thing is to get an even weight distribution in the candleholder, so that it doesn't tip over. Use trial and error. If it's too light, just add more beads. The galvanized wire is light and easy to work with, and when you add the glass prism at the bottom, the candleholder looks gorgeous.

Supplies needed:

Galvanized wire
Glass prism
Beads
Thin metal wire

What to do:

1 Wrap the galvanized wire around a small taper candle 5–6 times. The last time around make a ring so that the candle has something to stand on.

2 Shape the wire into a standing "S" to make the actual hook that will hang on the branch of the tree.

3 Let the wire hang approximately 8 in and finish with a hook that you can fasten the prism to.

4 Wind the thin metal wire a few times around the galvanized wire, starting by the hook.

5 Thread a few beads onto the metal wire and wrap them around the galvanized wire, repeating until you have a bunch of beads. Wrap the metal wire a few extra times to fasten it.

6 Hang the prism together with some beads on a little bit of thin metal wire and attach the wire to the loop.

7 Check carefully to make sure that your candle holder is balanced before you hang it in the tree with a lit candle. Never leave burning candles unsupervised.

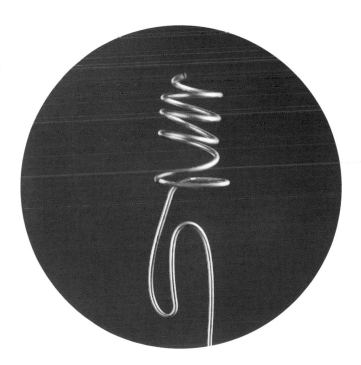

Molding candles

I think making your own candles is a beautiful and enjoyable tradition. If you find it too difficult to dip candles on your own, you might prefer to try the molding technique. Gather the family for a cozy Christmas crafts night. While you're already at the stove watching the wax, you might as well make some Christmas goodies together.

You'll find all the supplies you need for making candles in the paint and craft stores. It's important to melt the wax in a water bath and not let it get too hot. Read the instructions carefully for the wax you buy. Here I've used an old metal tureen mold—candles in different shapes are always fun. If you use large molds you should give each mold two wicks. Another good mold is an ordinary tin can.

Supplies needed:
Wax
Melting pot with handles
Cooking pot
Candle wicks
Skewers or florist sticks
Adhesive putty
Mold
Aluminum foil

What to do:
1 Pour the wax into a melting pot and place it in a water bath inside a second pot on the stove.

2 Allow it to melt at medium heat.

3 Tie candle wicks to wooden sticks and fasten them to the bottom of the mold with a bit of adhesive putty.

4 Pour the melted wax carefully into the mold.

5 Place aluminum foil on top of the mold and allow the candle to cool.

Festive ideas

Personally I think Christmas is the most festive holiday of the year. But it's only what you make of it, so it's well worth it to devote a little extra energy to togetherness. Take the time to be with your loved ones and take care of one another.

Children's apron

One beloved tradition in our home is the Christmas baking. We almost never bake otherwise, but at Christmas it's a requirement. We make everything from saffron buns to gingerbread cookies to German-inspired Christmas stollen. Naturally this takes some time, but it's worth every minute. The children just love helping with the sweets for Christmas, and we have a very cozy and pleasant time as we crowd into the kitchen.

To protect their clothes from spots, I've sewn aprons for my kids. For best results, use a cotton material so that you can wash it easily. Here I've sewn the apron inside out to make it nice and firm. You'll find the pattern for the apron on page 96. Enlarge it as needed to fit the size of the baker.

Supplies needed:

Cotton fabric
Scissors and pins
French chalk and sewing thread
Pattern paper and pen
Measuring tape

What to do:

1 Enlarge the pattern from page 96 onto pattern paper and cut it out.

2 Pin the pattern to the fabric and cut out two parts, so that the apron will be doubled.

3 Cut fabric strips for the ties: two sized 21.6 × 3.9 in (55 × 10 cm) and two sized 39.4 × 3.9 in (100 × 10 cm).

4 Sew the strips together inside out, trim the seam allowance and turn them right side out, poke out the corners, and smooth them out.

5 Place the apron parts face to face and pin the strips between them. (Remember that the strips should be pinned upside down between the apron faces so that they will look right when you reverse the apron parts.)

6 Sew the pieces together with a straight seam using a sewing machine. Leave an opening of 3.9 in (10 cm).

7 Trim the seam allowance and cut the corners diagonally.

8 Turn the apron right side out, poke out the corners, and press out the seams.

9 Sew the opening together by hand.

Host gifts

When invited to someone's home, it's customary to bring something nice for the hosts. Usually we come bearing flowers or a bottle of wine. Although these gifts are appreciated, sometimes a little creativity is nice. You can fill this can with anything from homemade toffees to exotic nuts.

From ordinary tin cans you can make pretty containers. They are perfect for keeping goodies in. Seal them with a pretty fabric, a thin silk ribbon, and—as a finishing touch—a painted wooden heart. Feel free to paint the outside of the can with water-based craft paint, allow it to dry, and repeat until the surface is completely covered. You can find the wooden button in a craft store; it too can be painted in a matching color. Thread the thin silk ribbon through the wooden button, and the can is done!

Three napkin rings

I think setting the table for a party is important for establishing a theme. Choose a style for your Christmas table, and then start creating. It's a special feeling to sit down at a beautifully set table; it immediately makes the dinner more festive. It really doesn't have to be very complicated—with a few pretty napkin rings you'll go far.

You can make a very simple napkin ring from a pretty velvet ribbon. Use a color that matches the rest of your table setting. For every napkin you will need approximately 20 inches of ribbon. Then you just have to roll the napkin and tie a classic bow around it. It can hardly get any simpler!

This is a fun napkin ring to make; it's made of thick felt and suits many different table settings. Felt is "in" again, so it's easy to get a hold of and comes in many pretty colors. Check your craft or fabric store. You will also need a matching button and string. Cut the felt to 6.7 × 2.4 in (17 × 6 cm) in size. Sew on a button 1.2 in (3 cm) from one of the short edges. Cut the string 15.7 in (40 cm) long and fold it halfway. Thread the string double on a sewing needle and poke it through the felt .4 in (1 cm) from the edge on the other short side. Tie a double knot so the string stays in place. Now you just have to roll the napkin, wrap the felt around it, and anchor it by wrapping the string a few times around the button.

A pretty napkin ring, filled with Christmasy red beads in all shapes. This is a napkin ring that the children like to help make. In the craft store you'll find many pretty and fun beads to use—everything from small traditional ones to heart-shaped ones. It's also nice to use sequins together with the beads. Cut a red metal wire, 25.6 in (65 cm) long, and make a hook at one end. Thread the beads and the sequins onto the wire and finish by twisting the ends together.

Fabric cones

These cones are just as practical as they are decorative. You can either keep Christmas goodies in them or just fill them with some eye candy. Hang them right on the wall, door knob, or why not in the tree? This is also a nice and much appreciated present to fill with a little of everything and give to your hosts if you're invited to someone's home. If you want the cone to be able to hold more, just make a larger size.

Adapt the hanger on the cone according to how you want to hang it, such as with a loop or a ribbon. Feel free to decorate the cone in your own way; one of the cones here has a pom-pom at the end. Reinforce the material by ironing on interfacing on the back side. Trim the edges of the cone with matching fabric. You can hang the cone with either a satin ribbon or the same fabric as in the trim. You'll find the pattern on the pattern pages.

Supplies needed:

Cotton fabric
Interfacing
Fabric for trimming edges
Ribbon for hanging
A pom-pom (optional)
Scissors
Pins
Pen
Tracing paper

What to do:

1 With a warm iron, press the interfacing to the back side of the cotton fabric.

2 Transfer the cone pattern from page 96 to the fabric and cut it out.

3 Place the two sides of the cone together, pin, and sew them together by machine.

4 Trim the point and the seam allowance.

5 Turn the cone right side out and poke out the corner with scissors or a similar implement.

6 Pin and sew trim around the opening of the cone.

7 Sew a ribbon or a loop on either side of the opening.

8 If desired, you can sew a cotton pom-pom to the point of the cone.

83

Christmas scrapbook

Save your Christmas memories in a personal and fun way. If you've never tried making a memory album or scrapbook, you really should. Once you've tried the technique, it can be hard to stop. The end result is a photo album that's beautiful and well-organized. From now on, it will be a joy to show your family albums. Take the opportunity to save small items you encounter on various special occasions. These can be anything from ticket stubs to seashells.

To get a lasting result that you can enjoy for many years, you should work with oxygen-free products as much as possible. For example, you should never glue a wooden object into your scrapbook. If you're the slightest bit uncertain about something, you can either wrap it in plastic or store it in a plastic pocket.

There are lots of fun accessories that you can use in your creations. The whole idea of the technique is to make personalized photo albums by taping and gluing photos and other memorabilia onto heavy card stock. Use an ordinary ring binder or get a more attractive album specially intended for scrapbooking.

A popular aid that most scrapbookers use is double-sided tape. This is available in various types; the simplest type is on a spool. You can also try double-sided mounting tape, which gives your album a striking effect. When you make scrapbooks, you'll get the best results if you use a craft knife instead of scissors.

Tips and techniques

When you're doing crafts, the most important thing of all (apart from getting into the Christmas spirit, of course) is to use the right tools. For example, there is nothing more irritating than trying to cut fabric with a pair of kitchen shears. The Christmas mood and inspiration can be destroyed in a second. Therefore, it's a good idea to obtain the right tools before you get started.

Work with a craft knife

When you're working with paper, for example, to make your personalized Christmas cards, a craft knife is a very useful tool. You can save quite a bit of money by starting with large sheets of paper instead of buying ready-folded Christmas cards. This way you have the freedom to come up with your own shapes for the Christmas cards. Just remember to stick to the most common measurements so that you can find envelopes to fit your cards. Of course, you can also make your own envelopes; it's not as hard as you might think. In the craft store, you'll even find easy-to-use plastic patterns for envelopes of different sizes.

To get nice straight edges for your paper projects, it's a distinct advantage to work with a craft knife. This is a special knife that you can buy in the craft store or a well-stocked paper store. The blade is replaceable and should be changed as soon as it gets dull. Remember that this is a sharp knife and definitely not something children should use.

When you work with a craft knife, it's important to use a cutting mat. There are special cutting mats in different sizes available where you buy your craft knife. You can even use a plastic cutting board as a cutting mat. Just make sure it's thoroughly clean so that you don't get unwanted spots on your paper projects.

If you're cutting straight lines, you must use a metal ruler; a plastic ruler can easily get ruined if you use it with the craft knife. Hold the craft knife straight and with a steady hand at a 90-degree angle to the cutting mat and cut slowly against the mat. Store the craft knife in a safe place where children can't get a hold of it. A good tip is to bury the knife blade in a wine cork or similar material, to minimize the risk that you will hurt yourself accidentally.

Different scissors

There is an abundance of scissors to choose from. It might seem unnecessary to have a bunch of different scissors lying around at home, but I promise you that it's worth it in the long run. They will last longer, and at the same time it will be much easier to make things if you have the right tools.

The two most important scissors in my personal opinion are fabric shears and scissors for cutting paper (of course, you also need a good pair of kitchen shears). There are a lot of different price categories for scissors; this is one place where it can be worth spending a little more for quality.

important to choose a sturdy paper. Remember to write the name and address clearly, so that they really will get to the recipient.

There's paper for all personalities, from music paper and lace paper to iridescent mother-of-pearl paper. You can make many things besides cards from your paper. Why not throw together some cones and Christmas crackers while you're already making Christmas cards?

Gather the whole family together so that everyone can help out. You can have a good time and get a lot done at the same time. It's a great way to welcome Christmas.

Pinking shears are used primarily to cut fabric. Use them on fabrics where you want a zigzag or to make pretty edges on felt decorations, etc. There's not much to say about fabric shears; they are available in all price ranges, from a couple of dollars to very expensive. You decide what level suits your wallet.

A medium-sized pair of craft scissors is always useful to have on hand. These are used to split string or cut tape, for example. Scissors for cutting paper are available in a range of sizes, so choose the scissors according to what they will be used for. When you are cutting small patterns, it's easier if you use a small pair of pointy scissors so that you can easily follow the curves.

To give pretty and fun edges to your paper you can get pattern scissors. There are several different patterns to choose from, and they are often sold in sets in the craft store.

Paper

If you, like me, have a weakness for paper, it can be hard to make a decision, because there is such an incredible variety of paper to choose from, particularly the handmade kinds with lots of texture and personality. Even the transparent papers have become much more diverse and are now available in a lot of different patterns and colors.

When you are making Christmas cards and planning to send them without envelopes, it's

Tape and glue

Attaching different papers and materials to each other doesn't sound too difficult. All you have to do is watch the children when they need to put something together. They can use several feet of tape to put one poster on the wall. It's creative but, to be honest, not very attractive. These days, there are a lot of new and smart materials that make the work both simpler and more attractive. There is essentially a tape or glue for everything.

A very useful aid for making your own Christmas decorations and cards is double-sided tape. There are also double-sided adhesive sheets, which are sold in different sizes. One 8½ × 11 in sheet is enough for several products. Cut the sheet into whatever sized pieces you need. When the protective paper is removed, you have a good, strong double-sided tape. With this, you can make lots of fun things; just look at the children's glittery cards, for example.

If you want to be really efficient and fast, you can use double-sided tape on a roll. It's easy to stretch it along the material to be attached. Press it together, and it's stuck.

Another fun aid that creates a striking 3-D feeling is double-sided mounting tape. It's available in different varieties, such as a roll or small squares.

There are also lots of different varieties of glue, ranging from ordinary paper glue to glue that's specially adapted for glass or porcelain. It's important to choose the right glue for the material and goal. If you are gluing together sheets of paper, it's actually best to use the double-sided tape, at least if you want a lasting and attractive result. The paper glue can sometimes shrink up, and then the paper won't stay smooth.

In any case, it's a good idea to place the finished cards in a press, unless of course you've used mounting tape or other raised decorations.

If you don't want the hassle of obtaining glue for different kinds of materials, multipurpose (craft) glue is a good alternative. It works for most materials, but the drying time can range from material to material depending on the absorption capacity.

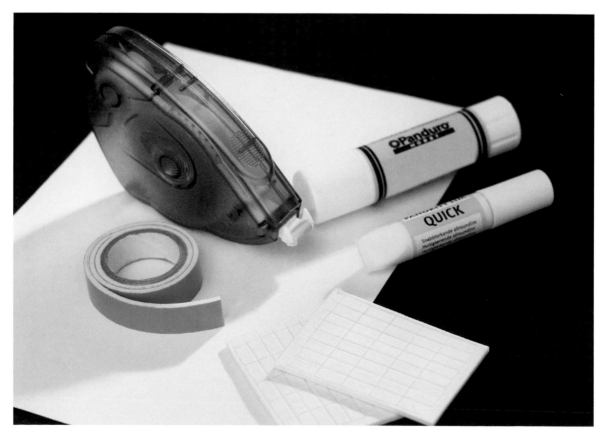

Glitter and glamour

At Christmastime, it feels right to glitter a little more. There are different kinds of glitter, both in loose and solid form. You can decorate with glitter in many ways, the easiest of which is to use glitter glue, which sticks to most materials. The loose glitter is probably the kind that gives the maximum glitter effect. Sprinkle some glitter in glue or varnish, or use double-sided adhesive sheets.

The classic gold and silver pens never go out of style. It's always attractive to write Christmas greetings with a festive color. Choose between different widths—if you want an attractive script you can get the best results by using a pen with a calligraphy point.

Writing and decorating with glaze pens can be very striking because the text is raised. Write slowly with the pens so that you get enough "ink" to create the relief effect. The pens are available in many colors, with or without metallic gloss.

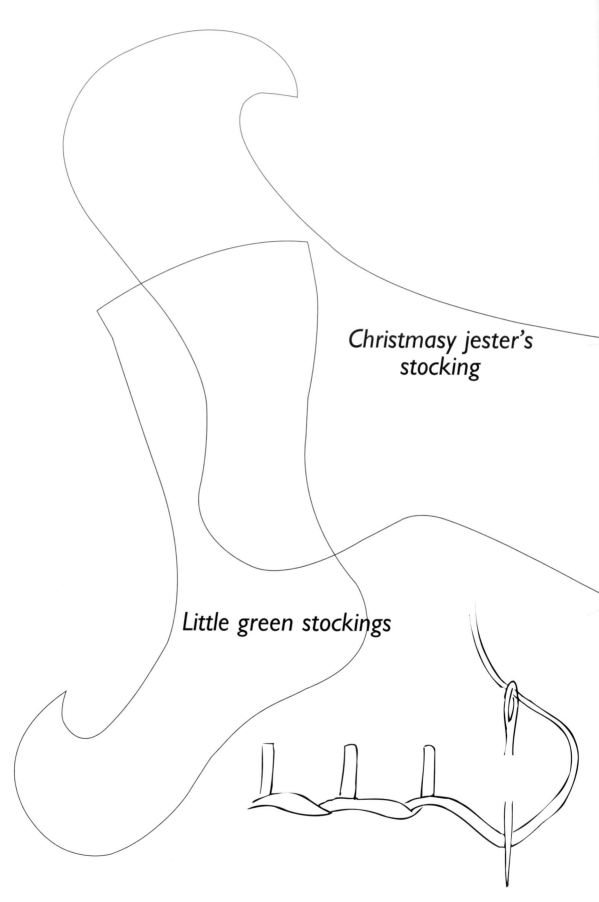

Christmasy jester's stocking

Little green stockings

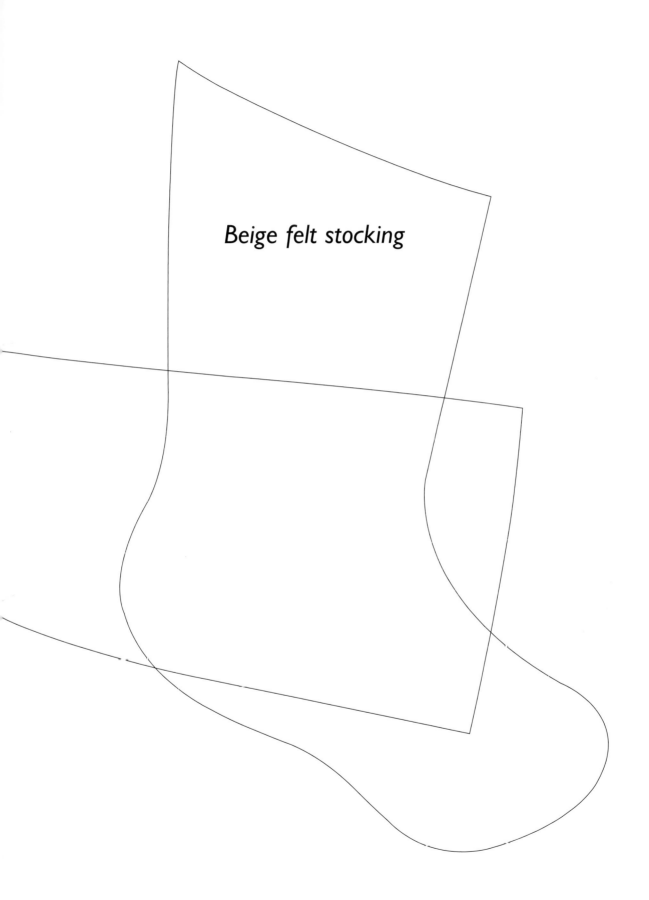

Beige felt stocking

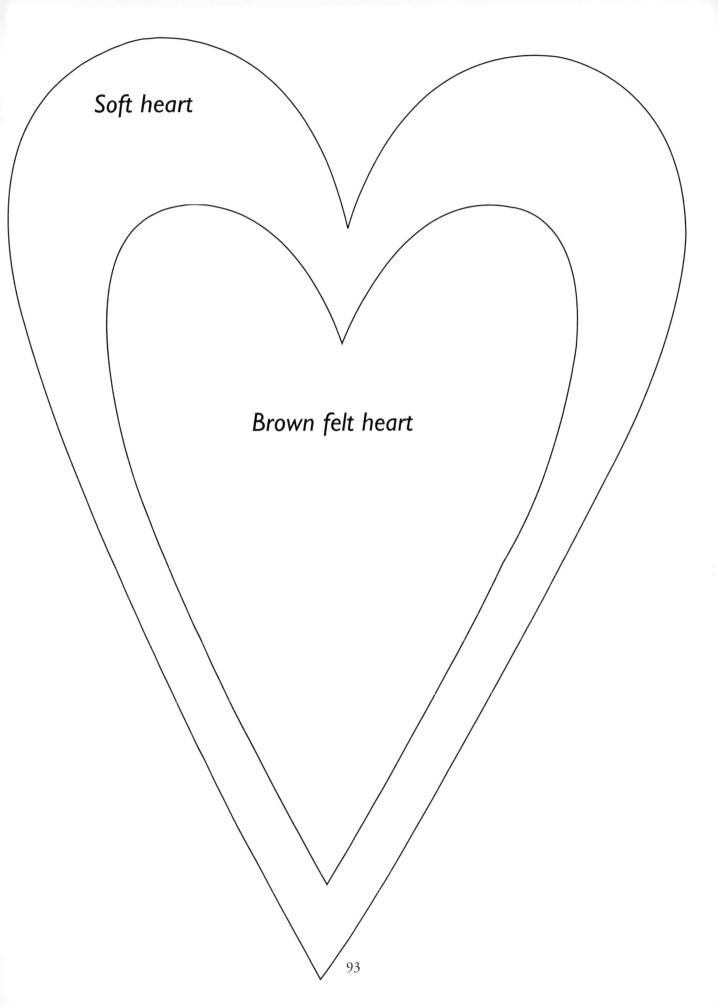

Soft heart

Brown felt heart

93

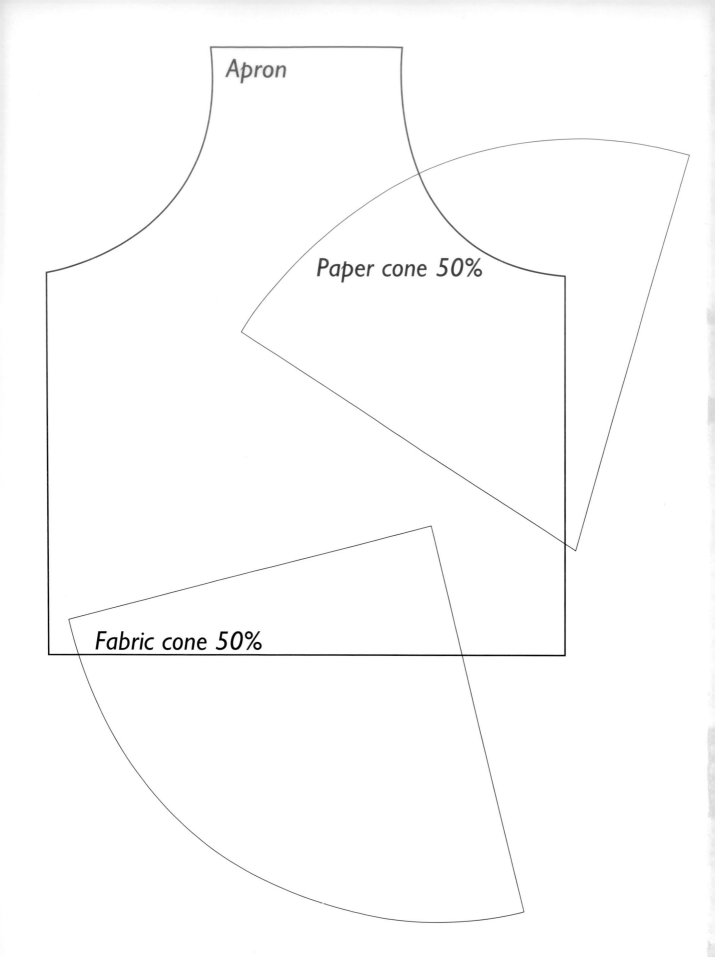

Apron

Paper cone 50%

Fabric cone 50%